The Renaissance

Susie Brooks

COMPASS POINT BOOKS
a capstone imprint

Compass Point Books are published by Capstone,
1710 Roe Crest Drive, North Mankato, Minnesota 56003
www.mycapstone.com

Library of Congress Cataloging-in-Publication Data
Title: The Renaissance / by Susie Brooks.
Description: North Mankato, Minnesota : Compass Point Books, a Capstone
   imprint, [2020] | Series: Inside art movements | Audience: 9-14. |
   Audience: 4 to 6.
Identifiers: LCCN 2018060767 | ISBN 9780756562397 (hardcover)
Subjects: LCSH: Art, Renaissance—Juvenile literature.
Classification: LCC N6370 .B76 2020 | DDC 709.02/4–dc23
LC record available at https://lccn.loc.gov/2018060767

Editorial credits
Series editor: Julia Bird
Designer: Mo Choy Design Ltd.
Image research: Diana Morris

Image credits:
Front cover. Raphael, Lady with a Unicorn, c.1505, oil on panel, now on canvas, 65 x 61 cm, Galleria Borghese, Rome. The Yorck Project/PD/Wikimedia Commons. 1. Raphael, Lady with a Unicorn, c.1505, oil on panel, now on canvas, 65 x 61 cm, Galleria Borghese, Rome. The Yorck Project/PD/Wikimedia Commons. 3. Hieronymus Bosch, right panel of Garden of Earthly Delights, Hell, c.1503-1515, part of triptych, oil on oak panel, 220 x 97.5 cm, Museo del Prado, Madrid. PD/Wikimedia Commons. 4t. Laocoön and his Sons, c.27 BCE-68 CE, marble, 208 x 163 x 112cm, Vatican Museums, Vatican City. binio/Shutterstock. 4b. Titian, Bacchus and Ariadne, 1520-1523, oil on canvas, 176.5 x 191 cm, National Gallery, London. Artepics/age fotostock/Superstock. 5. Leonardo, The Lady with an Ermine, Portrait of Cecilia Gallerani, oil and tempera on wood panel, 54.8 x 40.3 cm, Muzeum Czartoyskich, Krakow. PD/Wikimedia Commons. 6. Cimabue, Maesta di Santa Trinita,1290-1300, tempera on wood panel, 385 x 223 cm, Galleria degli Uffizi, Florence. Google art project/Wikimedia Commons. 7. Giotto, The Betrayal of Christ (Kiss of Judas), c.1306, fresco, 200 x 185 cm, Scrovengni Chapel, Padua. PD/Wikimedia Commons. 8-9. Ambrogio Lorenzetti, The Effects of Good Government,1338-9, fresco, approx 200 cm x 1372cm, Civic Museum and Mangia Tower, Siena. Google Cultural Institute/PD/Wikimedia Commons. 10bl. Ghiberti, self-portrait. Detail from Gates of Paradise, East side, Baptistry of San Giovanni, Florence, 1425-52, gilded bronze relief. Richardfabi/CC Wikimedia Commons. 10r. Ghiberti, Gates of Paradise, Baptistry of San Giovanni, Florence, 1425-52, gilded bronze relief, 5 06 x 287 cm. Saliko/CC Wikimedia Commons. 11tl. Ghiberti, Christ walks on Water, panel 8, North side door, Baptistry of San Giovanni, Florenze, 1401-22, gilded bronze relief, 52.07 x 45.01 cm. De Agostini/Getty Images. 11tr. Ghiberti, Joseph panel from Gates of Paradise, Baptistry, Florence,1425-52, gilded bronze relief, 79.4 x 79.4cm. vvoe/Shutterstock. 11b.Brunelleschi, Duomo, Cattedrale di Santa Maria del Fiore, Firenze, completed 1436. Anton Ivanov/Shutterstock. 12. Masaccio, The Holy Trinity, 1426, fresco, 667 x 317 cm Santa Maria Novella, Florence. De Agostini/Superstock. 13t. Masaccio, The Payment of the Tribute, 1426-7, fresco, 247 x 597 cm. Brancacci Chapel, Santa Maria del Carmine, Florence. Eugene a/ CC Wkipedia Commons. 13b. Uccello, Battle of San Romano, 1438-40, tempera on poplar panel, 182 x 320cm, National Gallery, London. A. Burkatovski/Fine art Images/Superstock. 14. Published by Philip Galle, A Painter's Workshop, 1595, engraving, Rijksprentenkabinet, Amsterdam. PD/Wikimedia Commons. 15t. Giovanni di Ser Giovanni (Lo Scheggia), Cassone Adimari, c.1450, tempera on wood panel, 85.5 x 303 cm, Galleria dell'Accademia, Florence. Eugene a/ CC Wkipedia Commons. 15bl. Verocchio, Tobias and the Angel, 1470-5, tempera on wood panel, 83.6 x 66cm, National Gallery, London. Universal Images/Superstock. 15cr. Ibid. detail of fish. Universal Images/Superstock. 15br. ibid. detail of dog. Universal Images/Superstock. 16. Jan Van Eyk, Arnolfini Marriage, 1434, oil on oak panel, 82.2 x 60 cm, National Gallery, London. Artepic/age fotostock/Superstock. 17. Robert Campin, The Mérode Altarpiece, c.1427-32, triptych, oil on oak panels, 64.5 x 117.8 cm, Metropolitan Museum of Art, New York. Google art project/PD/Wikimedia Commons. 18. The Discobolus Lancellotti, 2nd CE, Roman copy of Greek original by Myron, marble, h 124cm, Palazzo Massimo all Terme, Rome. Carole Raddato, Frankfurt/CC Wikimedia

Commons. 19t. Donatelllo, Equestrian statue of Gattamelata, 1453, bronze, 340 x 390 cm.P iazzo del Santo, Padua. Vladimir Korostyshevskiy/Dreamstime. 19b. Piero Pollaiuolo, Apollo and Daphne, 1470-80, oil on wood panel, 29.5 x 20 cm, National Gallery, London. De Agostini/Superstock 20.Botticelli, Primavera, 1477-82, tempera on wood panel, 20.3 x 31.4 cm, Galleria degli Uffizi, Florence. Google Cultural InstitutePD/Wikimedia Commons. 21. Antonio Canova, The Three Graces, 1814-17, marble, 173 x 97.2 x 57 cm, Victoria & Albert Museum, London. Slawek Kozakiewicz/Dreamstime. 22. Mantegna, Portrait of the Gonzaga Family, c.1470, fresco, 805 x 807 cm, Camera degli Sposi, Castel San Giorgio, Mantua. A Burkatovski/Fine Art Images/Superstock. 23. Ghirlandaio, Confirmation of the Rule, 1483-5, fresco, Sasetti Chapel, Santa Trinita, Florence. De Agostini/Superstock. 24. Marble Quarry at Carrara. Leon Vitti/Dreamstime. 25. Michelangelo, David, 1501-04, marble, h 517 cm, Galleria dell'Accademia, Florence. Leud2k/Dreamstime. 26. Leonardo, Portrait of Lisa Gherardini known as the Mona Lisa. c.1503-19., oil on poplar panel, 77 x 53 cm, Musée du Louvre, Paris. Dcoetzee/PD/Wikimedia Commons. 27. Raphael, Lady with a Unicorn, c 1505, oil on panel now on canvas, 65 x 61 cm, Galleria Borghese, Rome. The Yorck Project. PD/Wikimedia Commons. 28tl. Leonardo, presumed self-portrait, c 1512, red chalk on paper, 33.3 x 21.6 cm, Biblioteca Reale, Turin. Jakub Krechowicz/Shutterstock. 28r. Leonardo, Design for a tank and a flying machine,1493, 30 x 20 cm, pen and ink on paper. Science & Society PL/Superstock. 29tl. Leonardo, Anatomical study of the neck and shoulder, c. 1510-11, pen and ink on paper, 29.2 x 19.8 cm. The Royal Collection, Windsor. PD/Wikimedia Commons. 29br. Leonardo, Study of Five Grotesque Heads, c.1494, pen and ink on paper, 26 x 20.5 cm, The Royal Collection, Windsor. Ilbusca/Istockphoto. 30. Raphael, The School of Athens, c.1511, fresco, 500 x 770 cm. The Apostolic Chapel, Vatican City. PD/Wikimedia Commons. 31t. ibid. three details. 31b. Raphael, Portrait of Pope Julius II, 1511, oil on poplar panel, 108 x 81 cm, National Gallery, London. Peter Barritt/Superstock. 32t. Michelangelo, Ceiling of the Sistine Chapel, 1508-12, fresco, 40 x 14m, Vatican City. RPBaiao/Shutterstock. 32b. Michelangelo, Cartoon of the Libyan Sibyl, c.1510-11, red, white & black chalk on paper, 28.9 x 21.4 cm, Metropolitan Museum, New York. PD/Metmus. 33. Michelangelo, The Creation of Adam, detail from Sistine Chapel ceiling, 1508-12, fresco, Vatican City. Creative Lab/Shutterstock. 34. Bellini, Doge Leonardo Loredan, 1501, oil on wood panel, 62 x 45 cm, National Gallery, London. Peter Barritt/Superstock. 35bl. Titian, Doge Andrea Gritti, 1545, oil on canvas, 134 x 103 cm, National Gallery of Art, Washington. Fototeca Gilardi/Marka/Superstock. 35tr. Giorgione, The Tempest, 1506 oil on canvas, 83 x 73, Galleria dell' Accademia, Venice. PD/Wikimedia Commons. 36. Albrecht Dürer, The Rhinoceros, 1515, , woodcut, 23.5 x 29.8 cm. PD/Wikimedia Commons. 37. Albrecht Dürer, Self Portrait,1500, Alte Pinakothek, Munich, oil on wood panel,67.1 x 48.9 cm, National Gallery of Art, Washington. Fooh2107/CC Wikimedia Commons. 38. Hieronymus Bosch, Garden of Earthly Delights, c.1503-1515, triptych, oil on oak panels, 220 x 389 cm, Museo del Prado, Madrid. PD/Wikimedia Commons. 39t. Hans Holbein the Younger, The Ambassadors, 1533, oil on oak panel, 207 x 209.5 cm. National Gallery, London. Peter Barritt/Superstock. 39b. Pieter Breugel the Elder, Children's Games, c. 1560, oil on wood panel,118 x 161 cm, Kunsthistorisches Museum, Vienna. CQEeZWQPO12Yjg at Google Cultural Institute/PD/Wikimedia Commons. 40. Parmigianino, Madonna with the Long Neck, 1535, oil on wood panel, 219 x 135 cm, Galleria degli Uffizi, Florence. gAEsEn4eJXVHyg at Google Cultural Institute/PD/Wikimedia Commons. 41. El Greco, The Annunciation, 1596-1600, oil on canvas,113 x 65 cm, Museo de Bellas Artes, Bilbao. 7gE1r9-kd352kg at Google Cultural Institute/PD/Wikimedia Commons. 42.Sofonisba Anguissola, Game of Chess, 1555, oil on canvas, 72 x 97 cm, Muzeum Narodwe, Poznan. poster.us.com/PD/Wikimedia Commons. 43t. Levina Teerlinc, Princess Elizabeth Tudor, c.1550, miniature, waterolour on vellum, h 5cm, Yale Center for British Art. PD/Wikimedia Commons. 43b. Fede Galizia, Still Life c. 1607, oil on wood panel, 31 x 42 cm, Private Collection. PD/Wikimedia Commons. 44bl. Picasso, Seated Woman, 1920, oil on canvas, 92 x 65 cm, Musée Picasso, Paris. © Succession Picasso/DACS London 2018. A Bukoatovski/Fine Art Images/Superstock. 44tr. Caravaggio, The Calling of St Matthew c. 1600, oil on canvas, 322 x 340 cm, San Luigi de Francesi, Rome. PD/Wikimedia Commons. 45. Andy Warhol, Colored Mona Lisa, 1963, silkscreen inks & graphite on canvas, 319.7 x 208.6 cm, Private Collection. © 2018 The Andy Warhol Foundation for Visual Arts, Inc./Licensed by DACS, London. Christies Images/Bridgeman Images.

First published in Great Britain in 2018 by Wayland
Copyright © Hodder & Stoughton, 2018

All internet sites appearing in back matter were available and accurate when this book was sent to press.

Printed and bound in China.
1593

Table of Contents

Art Reborn

Giant marble sculptures that seem alive, paintings you could step right into . . . these are two things the Renaissance is famous for. This period of great creativity, beginning in Italy around six hundred years ago, has influenced art ever since.

Ancient and New

The term Renaissance means "rebirth," and it refers to a time in Europe between the early 1400s and mid-1500s. During this era, people revived the ideas of ancient Greece and Rome. Artists developed techniques, such as perspective, that helped them to make incredibly realistic paintings and sculptures. They celebrated the beauty of nature and the human form.

Laocoön and his Sons, sculptors of Rhodes, c. 40–30 BCE

Bacchus and Ariadne, Titian, c.1520–23

Classical Style

In Italy people began remembering the glory of the Roman Empire. They read classical texts, studied sculptures such as the *Laocoön* (above), and painted scenes from myths, such as the painting at left of the god Bacchus and the goddess Ariadne by Tiziano Vecellio (Titian). Before this, art mainly served a religious purpose, and paintings looked flat and decorative. Renaissance artists were determined to move on (and look back) to something more monumental.

Crossing the Continent

Artistic skills were developing in northern Europe too. Here painters discovered they could make highly detailed, realistic works using oil paints. Around the same time in Germany, the invention of the large-scale printing press helped ideas to spread across the continent. Books hit the streets, and a new era of literacy and learning began.

Artist Celebrities

At the beginning of the Renaissance, artists were regarded as ordinary craftsmen. But backed by wealthy patrons, Leonardo da Vinci, Michelangelo Buonarroti, Raffaelo Santi (Raphael), Titian, and others reached celebrity status. Da Vinci's *Lady with an Ermine* (below) is just one example of this artist's remarkable ability to breathe life into his painting. Images like this have become iconic in today's world.

Lady with an Ermine, Leonardo da Vinci, 1485–90

Church and Change

For hundreds of years before the Renaissance, life in Europe was ruled by the powerful Catholic Church. Most work for artists involved decorating religious buildings. Although this continued, in the 14th century new ideas bubbled up.

Medieval Style

In medieval times leading up to the Renaissance, the Church commissioned images that helped people learn about Christianity. These included wooden panel paintings called altarpieces, like the *Maestá* by Cenni di Pepi (Cimabue) below. They were stylized and ornate, often using expensive materials such as gold leaf. As religious symbols, they didn't try to reflect the real world.

Signs of Space

Cimabue's work is interesting because it shows signs of change. The subject of Jesus and his mother Mary surrounded by saints is typically medieval, as is the gold and the decorative style. But while the figures seem stiff and relatively flat, there are attempts to create a sense of space. We get some feeling that Mary is sitting on a solid throne.

Look Closer

How has Cimabue tried to suggest depth? Notice the lines of the throne and the way the figures are colored and positioned.

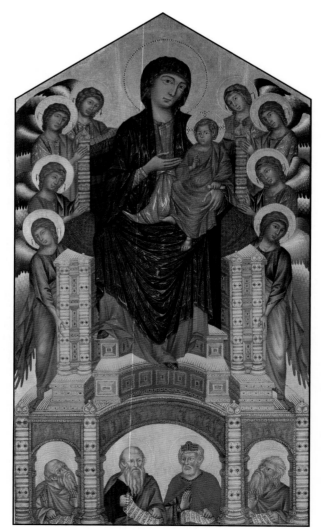

Santa Trinita Maestá (Virgin and Child with Prophets), Cimabue, c. 1290–1300

Human Emotion

Giotto di Bondone was a pupil of Cimabue in Florence. He took steps beyond his teacher in shading his figures for a three-dimensional effect and giving them individual expressions. Notice the characters in the fresco below—they look animated and active. Giotto was praised for rescuing art from medieval "darkness" and moving back toward the naturalism of ancient Rome.

Betrayal of Christ (Kiss of Judas), Giotto, 1304–06

Losing Faith

The idea that people are individuals in charge of their own destiny was emerging at the time in a school of thought called humanism. It marked a shift in interest from spiritual ideas to humans and their emotions. This was partly driven by a loss of faith in the Catholic Church, as people began to see the Church leaders as more intent on making money than giving religious guidance.

A **Scene** in Siena

Well-dressed women dance in a circle, shopkeepers happily sell their wares, donkeys carry bulging sacks of grain from the countryside . . . this panoramic fresco shows us a city prospering thanks to good government.

A Wealthy State

Ambrogio Lorenzetti painted this idyllic scene on the wall of the town hall in Siena. In those days, Italy was not a unified nation but a collection of city states, each run like a country in itself. Siena was one of the wealthier states, and its rulers held meetings in this room. The fresco was meant to remind them what they could achieve by being fair and good.

Idyllic Detail

Lorenzetti included a lot of detail! In the bustling city, you can see shops selling clothes and food, students in a lesson, people peeping through windows, and builders working on the rooftops. Over in the countryside, a group of noblemen set off hunting while a peasant brings a pig to market. Farmers are sowing and harvesting crops out in the fields.

A Real Scene

This obviously isn't a religious painting but a view of the earthly world. It marks a time when rich dukes and merchants were gaining power over the pope and the Catholic Church. Not only was it one of the first large secular (nonreligious) works, but it also looks like the actual landscape of Siena. This type of real-life observation was new and unusual for the time.

Fresco Technique

Painting a fresco like this took preparation. First the wall had to be smoothed with layers of plaster, then the artist would sketch out his scene. While the plaster was still damp, he would add the color using water-based pigments that fixed as the plaster dried. If the artist made a mistake, he had to cut that section out and start again!

The Effects of Good Government in the City and the Country, Ambrogio Lorenzetti, 1338

Flourishing Florence

Of all the Italian city states, 15th-century Florence was the biggest and richest. It had bounced back after decades of plague and warfare to become a leading trade center, packed with scholars and talented craftsmen. The Renaissance flourished in Florence.

Rule of the Guilds

Florence was governed by rich merchant families and guilds. To work in any particular craft or profession, you had to be a member of a guild. These powerful trade organizations competed with each other for status and often commissioned great art to help promote themselves.

Competition Time

In 1401 the Cloth Merchants Guild held a contest to design some doors for the Florence Baptistery. The winner was Lorenzo Ghiberti, a sculptor and goldsmith. His work was such a hit that the guild soon ordered another set of doors, occupying Ghiberti for much of the rest of his life. You can see why Michelangelo later named them the "Gates of Paradise."

Gates of Paradise, Lorenzo Ghiberti, 1425–52

Self-portrait of Ghiberti from the *Gates of Paradise*

Worlds in Bronze

Ghiberti's doors (above) were cast in bronze, which would have been extremely expensive! In the *Gates of Paradise* panels, he created detailed worlds that you can look right into, like windows. This is relief sculpture, projecting from a flat surface–but the foreground parts are almost fully 3D. Further back, they get shallower until they are simply etched in line.

▶

Look Closer

Compare these two panels from Ghiberti's earlier and later doors. Can you see the difference? In his later work, Ghiberti explored the recent development of perspective (see below).

Brilliant Brunelleschi

Filippo Brunelleschi, a goldsmith and sculptor too, lost out to Ghiberti in the Baptistery contest. After that, he turned to architecture and stunned people with his Florence Cathedral Dome (Duomo). This astonishing feat of engineering was achieved without even using scaffolding! Brunelleschi also devised a system that would revolutionize art–linear perspective.

Brunelleschi's Duomo (completed in 1436) dominates the Florence skyline.

A Sense of Space

We all know that paintings are flat, not three-dimensional. But when Brunelleschi developed perspective, he gave artists a way to fool the viewer—to create the illusion of space and distance on a two-dimensional surface.

Vanishing Point

Brunelleschi noticed that when we look at something going into the distance–a train track, for example–the parallel lines eventually seem to meet up. They join at a single point on the horizon, known as the vanishing point. Brunelleschi used this idea and other calculations to paint a very accurate view of the Florence Baptistery.

Alberti's Grid

In 1435 the scholar Leon Battista Alberti explained how to use perspective in a book for painters. To help, he described a drawing gridmade by stretching threads across a wooden frame. Looking at their subject through the grid, the artist could copy what they saw in each square onto a similar grid on his paper or canvas.

Amazing Alcove

Tommaso Cassai (Masaccio) was one of the first Renaissance painters to truly master perspective. You can see the depth in his Holy Trinity fresco (right), which looks like a real alcove high up in the chapel wall. Before he painted it, Masaccio used a nail and strings to mark the vanishing point and perspective lines. They all converge at the viewer's eye level, at the base of the cross.

The Holy Trinity, Masaccio, 1426

Artists often put important features at the vanishing point of their paintings. Can you see how the lines of the architecture and landscape below lead toward Christ's head?

Payment of the Tribute Money, Masaccio, c. 1425–27

Perspective Battle

Paolo Uccello would stay up all night worrying about perspective! In this battle scene (below), he deliberately angled broken lances on the ground towards the vanishing point. He also demonstrated how people and objects appear smaller the further away they are. And he foreshortened the fallen warrior (bottom left), showing how things look squatter if you view them from one end.

Battle of San Romano, Paolo Uccello, 1438–40

The Artist's Workshop

Artists were very busy during the Renaissance. Their commissions varied from grand public murals to decorating shields, fountains, furniture, and more. Master artists ran busy workshops where they trained apprentices in their craft.

Joint Effort

Look back to Ghiberti's Baptistery doors–they were not a one-man job! His assistants included Donato di Niccolo di Betto Bardi (Donatello) and Uccello. Every great Renaissance artist learned through the workshop system. Most large-scale works were collaborations between a master artist and his trainees.

A Renaissance artist's workshop

The Apprentice

Apprentices usually began at a young age, around 11 or 12. They worked at grinding pigments and preparing panels before learning to draw. Once they were accomplished painters, they took on minor parts of commissions, always in their master's style. They only became artists in their own right when they had a work accepted by the guild.

Making Paints

Renaissance artists did not have ready-made paints. Apprentices had the task of preparing powdered pigments, extracting color from earth, stone, wood, plants, and even bones or insects. Creating some colors, such as ultramarine blue from the gem lapis lazuli, involved lengthy, painstaking work. Once the pigments were ground and ready, they were mixed with a binder.

Adimari Cassone, Giovanni di Ser Giovanni, c. 1440

Wedding Panel

Furniture and interiors were often the items that kept art workshops in business. Giovanni di Ser Giovanni, brother of Masaccio, painted this narrow panel for either a wedding chest or the walls of a bridal chamber. It is rich in detail, showing the wealthy couple and their party. You can see that an interest in perspective ran in this artist's family!

Tobias and the Angel, Andrea del Verrocchio, 1470–75

Look Closer

The fish and dog in this painting (above) by Verrocchio are thought to be the work of his most famous pupil, Leonardo da Vinci. Can you see differences between them and other parts of the scene?

Mastering Oils

For hundreds of years, artists who decorated wooden panels had only one choice of paint—tempera. While this continued in early Renaissance Italy, northern European artists were developing something new—oil paints.

An Old New Medium

Oil paint was used as long ago as the 7th century in parts of Asia, but from the 1400s its popularity rocketed in Europe. Artists in the Netherlands discovered that mixing pigments with linseed oil rather than water-based binders gave them a paint that dried very slowly. Tempera, which artists mixed with egg yolk, dried fast.

Tempera Versus Oil

To correct a mistake in tempera, artists had to paint over it. They could only work on one small area of a picture at a time, applying the paint in thin layers. With oils it was possible to blend and rework the paint days after applying it. A whole painting could be worked on at once and would last longer in cool, damp climates than tempera.

The Arnolfini Portrait, Jan van Eyck, 1434

Netherlandish Magic

Flemish painter Jan van Eyck was a magician with oils. He learned to layer the paint in thin glazes to build up deep, shimmering colors. This portrait of a newlywed couple shows his brilliance at capturing light effects and the complex textures of fabrics. For soft areas he would blend the paint with his fingers, adding minute detail elsewhere using brushes sometimes as fine as a single hair.

Angels and Mousetraps

Flemish artist Robert Campin painted this three-pieced panel, or triptych (below), with two assistants. The main image shows the angel Gabriel telling Mary that she will be the mother of Jesus. On the right we see Mary's carpenter husband Joseph, and on the left the owners of the painting kneel at the door. The whole scene is painted in great detail in oils. Interestingly, Campin set it in a contemporary home rather than biblical times.

The Mérode Altarpiece, Robert Campin,
c. 1427–32

Look Closer

Take some time to spot all the tiny details, from the mousetrap on Joseph's windowsill to the smoldering candle smoke. Do you notice anything about the use of space here too? Do you think this artist knew about perspective?

Ancient Ideals

Epic stories, magnificent buildings, beautiful statues, intellectual ideas . . . all these things inspired people in 15th-century Italy to look back to ancient times and relive the triumphs of Greek and Roman culture.

Real, but Ideal

One thing the ancients excelled at was sculpture. The Greeks set a tradition of heroic, often nude figures cast in bronze or carved in stone. They were particularly concerned with human proportion, which they idealized to look as perfect as possible. Roman copies of Greek statues like Myron's *Discobolus* (right) reveal an interest in dynamic poses too.

Golden Ratio

The Greeks based their ideal proportions on a precise "golden ratio," where the distance from ground to navel was 1.618 times the distance from the navel to the top of the head. They used this ratio for beauty in their architecture as well. Renaissance artists studied it and applied it to their own work, but they also studied anatomy, making their figures more realistic.

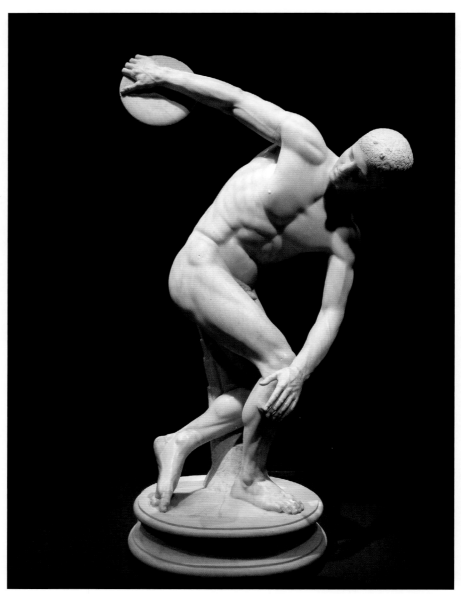

Roman copy of *Discobolus*

Colossal Horse

Huge public sculptures glorified ancient cities, and Renaissance leaders commissioned works to match. Donatello's vast bronze statue in Padua is similar to Roman equestrian monuments, but the lifelike feel and correct scale of horse to rider makes Donatello's work stand out. It amazed people by looking so natural, as well as for its technical skill.

Gattamelata, Donatello, 1453

Apollo and Daphne, Piero del Pollaiuolo, c. 1465

Magical Myths

The magical, mysterious world of classical myths soon appeared in Italian Renaissance work. Artists started painting Greek gods warring, celebrating, and courting. In the picture at left, Daphne the nymph is turning into a laurel to escape the god Apollo's affections. Behind them the landscape shows a valley close to Florence.

19

A Life-Size Myth

Women dressed in flowing robes dance in a blooming orange grove. The trees are laden with juicy fruits, and the ground is scattered with flowers. This is not a scene from a story but a painting that celebrates springtime.

Primavera, Sandro Botticelli, 1477–82

Giant Commission

Sandro Botticelli painted this panel above for the wealthy Medici family in Florence. It is difficult to know the exact meaning behind it, but we can decipher the main parts. The first thing to realize is that the painting is huge—the figures are all life-size. Mythical gods on this scale, some almost naked, had not been seen in art since ancient times.

Who Is Here?

In the center the Roman goddess Venus raises her hand in welcome. Her nephew Cupid is firing a flaming arrow above her head. On the far left Mercury swishes away a drifting cloud, while to the far right the floating Zephyr represents the spring breeze. As he breathes on the nymph Chloris, she turns into Flora, who sprinkles the world with flowers.

Look Closer

Venus is the focus of this springtime paradise. How does Botticelli make it clear that she is important? Look at her position and the colors he used.

Observing Nature

True to Renaissance principles, Botticelli really celebrated nature in this painting! Hundreds of types of plants have been counted here; there are even clusters of seeds on Mercury's sandals. Meanwhile the figures are idealized, with elongated arms. Their clothing and hair look light and delicate–this would have taken a lot of work in unforgiving tempera.

Three Graces

The ladies to the left of Venus are known as the Three Graces. Botticelli borrowed their pose from a type of classical sculpture that allowed the female figure to be viewed from several angles at once. You can see a later sculptor's version of the Three Graces below. Botticelli gave his trio a flowing sense of movement, as if they are dancing.

The Three Graces, Antonio Canova, 1814–17

Powerful Patrons

For artists to be successful in the Renaissance, they needed to attract wealthy patrons. A lot of work came from the governing families of Italy's city states, who commissioned art for their palaces and chapels.

Portrait of the Gonzaga Family, Andrea Mantegna, c. 1470

Tailor Made

Art was very much in demand during the Renaissance. Patrons commissioned art and paid for it. Artists rarely produced work for their own enjoyment or in the hope that it would sell. In this way, paintings and sculptures were usually tailored to suit the owner. They played an important part in shaping the public image of a ruler.

Court Artist

Andrea Mantegna worked for the ruling Gonzaga family in Mantua. As court artist, he helped to advertise their enormous wealth and power. This fresco is above a mantelpiece, so we look up to the figures, stressing their high status. Amazingly, all the architectural details over their heads are painted! This is known as trompe l'oeil, or "trick of the eye."

The Wealthy Medicis

The powerful Medici family of Florence were bankers, wool merchants, and generous patrons to the arts. Not only did they fill their buildings with paintings and sculptures, but Lorenzo de' Medici also set up an art school. Michelangelo started at the school at age 14 after an apprenticeship with Ghirlandaio. He was invited to live in the Medici home, where his great career began.

Confirmation of the Franciscan Rule, Domenico Ghirlandaio, 1483-6

Cameo Portraits

You can see a portrait of Lorenzo de' Medici with black hair on the right of this fresco by Ghirlandaio (above). It is a religious scene from the life of St. Francis—artists often incorporated images of their patrons and friends in paintings like this. The man in red next to Lorenzo is the banker Francesco Sassetti, who commissioned the work for a major church in Florence.

Magic in Marble

The colossal figure of a young, nude man stands confidently up on a pedestal. Made of solid marble, he weighs about as much as four small cars! Michelangelo spent over two years working in secret to sculpt this famous statue of David.

Giant in Stone

David (right) is as tall as a double-decker bus and was carved from a single block of marble. Imagine being faced with that enormous chunk of stone with only hand tools to transform it into a figure! Two sculptors had already tried and given up because the block was flawed and shallow–but the 26-year-old Michelangelo rose to the challenge.

Taking Shape

The biblical subject of David, the boy who slayed Goliath, had already been decided. But no one expected a sculptor to show David before battle, rather than victorious. Michelangelo began by making a wax model of his design, then he chipped away at the marble with a chisel. He worked tirelessly, day and night, until his stone *David* emerged, ready to fire his sling.

The vast block of marble came from the Cararra quarry, about 62 miles from Florence. Before sculpting could start, it had to be hacked out by hand, lowered down the mountain, and dragged along a river by oxen.

Almost Alive

We can see every muscle and sinew in this figure, including pulsing veins in the neck and hands. *David's* expression is alert as he stands with his weight on one leg—a pose called *contrapposto*, typical of classical art. The head and hands are unusually big. This was an intentional choice because the statue was meant to stand on the Florence Cathedral roofline, where its proportions would have made sense from below.

David, Michelangelo, 1501–04

Heroic Symbol

Michelangelo's *David* never made it to its intended position, but instead was hauled to the city's main square. This job took four days and 40 men, rolling the statue on tree trunks. Standing by the entrance to the Palazzo Vecchio, *David* became a heroic symbol of liberty and power in Florence. It was the biggest free-standing marble sculpture since ancient times.

▶ *Look Closer*

Michelangelo believed that every block of stone had a sculpture in it! Can you see how the shallow shape of this marble block dictated *David's* pose?

Color and Light

By the 1500s word had spread to Italy about the wonders of oil paints. Artists realized they could achieve exciting effects by glazing and blending. They explored the form-shaping qualities of light and shadows, giving their paintings extraordinary life.

Distant Haze

If you look at a stretch of open landscape, you can see that in the distance it seems paler. The far-off scenery loses its detail and takes on a hint of blue. Renaissance painters noticed this and translated it to their work. For example, the view shifts from clear to blue and hazy in the background of the *Mona Lisa* (right).

Mysterious Smile

Leonardo da Vinci's *Mona Lisa* is one of the most famous paintings in the world. People are intrigued by the woman's mysterious expression, which shows just a flicker of a smile. Leonardo used a technique called *sfumato*, or "smoky," where he softened the contrasts between light and dark. He blended paint at the corners of the mouth and eyes to make us uncertain of her mood.

Mona Lisa, Leonardo da Vinci, 1503–6

Renaissance Portraits

The *Mona Lisa* is thought to be a portrait of Lisa Gherardini, a Florentine merchant's wife. Stand-alone portraits were quite new in Renaissance Italy, but the half-length sitter, shown at a three-quarter degree angle, became a popular format. Artists often added a background window with a scenic view to give the painting extra depth.

Young Woman with Unicorn, Raphael, c. 1506

Raphael's Unicorn

No one is sure who the girl is in Raphael's painting, nor why she is holding a unicorn! X-rays show that originally Raphael painted a dog, but he changed it later, perhaps using the unicorn as a symbol of purity. Whatever the story, the portrait is elegant and lifelike, with light and shade, known as *chiaroscuro*, giving everything its shape.

Look Closer

Raphael was probably inspired by the *Mona Lisa*. Can you see similarities in the pose and setting of these two portraits? What about the differences? Which painting do you prefer?

The Renaissance Man

Arms stripped of their skin, revealing muscles, veins, and bones . . . complicated flying machines hovering in the air . . . these look a bit like textbook diagrams, but in fact they are pages from Leonardo da Vinci's many notebooks.

Presumed Self-Portrait, Leonardo da Vinci, c. 1510

Design For a Helicopter, Leonardo da Vinci, c. 1493

Great Inventions

Leonardo was a true genius of the Renaissance. He was brilliant at virtually everything, from art to engineering to geology. He designed war machines, calculators, bicycles, diving gear, and many other things that were way ahead of his time. His detailed vision for a helicopter (right) was made during an era when people traveled using horses or donkeys!

Mirror Writing

The pages of Leonardo's notebooks are covered in special shorthand written from right to left like mirror writing. This may have been to keep his ideas secret, or because he was left-handed and didn't want to smudge the ink. Either way, his notebooks help to give us an image of an all-round talent, or "Renaissance Man."

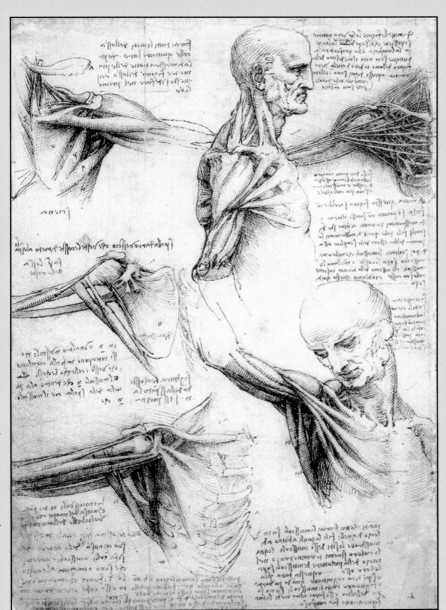

Studying Anatomy

One thing that particularly fascinated Leonardo was anatomy. In 1507 he dissected the body of an old man who had died in hospital, sketching in detail what he found (left). By the end of his life Leonardo had cut up more than 30 corpses and produced hundreds of anatomical drawings. He made groundbreaking discoveries about the human heart and produced the first accurate picture of a person's spine.

Study of Five Grotesque Heads,
Leonardo da Vinci, c. 1494

Curious Cartoons

Leonardo also studied living people. He walked the streets, seeking out characters to sketch—the more curious-looking the better. His pen-and-ink "grotesques" (right) are like caricatures with bulbous noses, sagging skin, and broken teeth. They are a far cry from the serene beauty of his *Mona Lisa*—one of fewer than 20 known paintings he made.

Rebirth in Rome

In the first two decades of the 16th century, the Italian city of Rome made a comeback. Its status had suffered while the popes spent a period based in France, but after decades of conflict they commissioned artists to help create a cultural capital of the world.

The School of Athens, Raphael, 1509–11

Decorating the Vatican

Raphael arrived in Rome in 1508, and was invited by Pope Julius II to decorate several rooms at the Vatican Palace. His fresco above shows great thinkers from ancient times—a true sign of the Renaissance, as it put human knowledge on equal footing with a religious scene that Raphael painted on the opposite wall.

Classic Composition

All the best-known classical philosophers and scientists are gathered in *The School of Athens*. The lines of perspective draw our eye straight to Plato and Aristotle in the center. The figures interact in groups, looking as natural as if we just stepped into a university hall. Raphael balanced the scene using golden ratios to position the archways and other important features.

Artist and Friends

Raphael included a self-portrait in *The School of Athens*–the young man in a black beret among a group of astronomers on the right. He also painted his rival Michelangelo as the philosopher Heraclitus, brooding alone in the foreground. The bearded Plato (background center left) is thought to be a portrait of Leonardo da Vinci.

Portrait of Pope Julius II, Raphael, 1511

Renaissance Rivals

Raphael painted this portrait at left during the High Renaissance–the period between 1490 and 1527 when artists reached new heights of skill and beauty in their work. Leonardo and Michelangelo were also High Renaissance masters. There was fierce competition between them all. Julius II encouraged this by employing both Raphael and Michelangelo at the Vatican.

Look Closer

Pope Julius II was a powerful figure who transformed Rome and waged war for control over Italian states. What mood has Raphael captured him in here?

A Very Famous Ceiling

Imagine painting all this detail on a surface nearly twice the size of a tennis court. Now imagine painting it on wet plaster—above your head—while standing awkwardly on scaffolding. That's how Michelangelo created the Sistine Chapel ceiling!

Sistine Chapel Ceiling, Michelangelo, 1508–12

Painting Up High

Working just around the corner from Raphael in the Vatican, Michelangelo began painting more than 65 feet above the ground. He worked up close, unable to see his progress from below because his scaffolding blocked the view. The frescoes show scenes from the Old Testament of the Bible, with more than 300 life-size figures telling the stories.

Preparatory Cartoons

Michelangelo made over 200 sketches for his ceiling. These were turned into cartoons—full-size drawings that artists often used to plan their fresco work (right). Every day, cartoons were laid on fresh plaster and traced with a pointed instrument called a stylus to transfer the design. Michelangelo then painted using colors bright enough to still be vivid down on the ground.

Statuesque Style

Michelangelo considered himself more a sculptor than a painter. You can see the influence of statues like the *Laocoön* (see page 4) in his muscly figures, twisting and turning at different angles. They interact in dramatic groups, weaving their way across the ceiling. The range of poses and expressions is impressive.

Four-Year Struggle

Famously temperamental, Michelangelo painted most of the ceiling alone after firing his assistants. He wouldn't let anybody in to watch him work. Some early parts of the fresco became moldy, forcing him to start again. It was four years before his efforts were unveiled and the ceiling began its rise to worldwide fame.

The Creation of Adam (detail from the Sistine Chapel ceiling), Michelangelo, 1508–12

Look Closer

Occasionally the younger Raphael crept in to see Michelangelo's progress. Do you think he was influenced? Look, for example, at the poses of figures in this work and *The School of Athens* on page 30.

Jewels of Venice

While artists battled in Renaissance Rome and Florence, others were emerging in Venice. This coastal city state, ruled by an elected doge, was rich from trade with Asia. It was teeming with artists and craftsmen who were rarely short of work.

City of Light

Being built beside water and crisscrossed by canals, Venice had a unique type of light. You might have noticed how colors glow and sparkle at the seaside. Venetian artists captured this jewellike effect. They worked in oils, which lasted longer in their damp climate than the frescoes still popular in drier Rome. Sometimes they mixed ground glass with their paint, to make it gleam even more.

Doge Leonardo Loredan, Giovanni Bellini, c.1501

Glowing Glazes

One of the first Venetian artists to take up oil paints was Giovanni Bellini. He used thin glazes like the artists in the Netherlands to make this painting of Doge Loredan (above) almost photographic. The portrait resembles a sculpted bust, popular in Roman times. It is stiff and upright, with luxurious clothing showing the importance of the sitter.

Atmospheric Color

Giorgione was a pupil of Bellini, but he used oils in a different way. There is much more sense of the thickness of paint in his painting *The Tempest* (right). Giorgione blended color to create atmosphere, conjuring up the moody feeling of a storm. The subject of his scene is uncertain, but this was one of the earliest Italian paintings to be called a landscape.

The Tempest, Giorgone, 1506–8

Doge Andrea Gritti, Titian, 1546

Dynamic Character

Of all the Venetian painters, Titian found the most fame. He filled his work with a new kind of energy, creating bright, dynamic compositions. Titian was also excellent at portraits showing personal character and expression. He won patrons across Italy and in Spain, painting the pope, doges, kings, and many other wealthy figures.

Look Closer

Titian made this portrait of Doge Andrea Gritti (above) as a memorial after he died. How does it compare to Bellini's portrait of Doge Loredan? Look at the brushwork, expression, and detail in the painting.

Renaissance Rhino

With a horn on its snout and armored skin, this looks like a rhinoceros–almost! When Albrecht Dürer made this woodcut, he had never seen a rhino and had only a few notes and sketches to guide him.

Strange Beast

In 1515 a rhinoceros arrived in Portugal from India as a gift for the king. It was the first rhino in Europe since Roman times, and people were amazed by what they saw. When Dürer heard news of this strange, horned animal, he was eager to draw it. He based his picture (below) on a description and sketch that were sent to his hometown, Nuremberg.

Northern Renaissance

Dürer lived in Germany which, along with the Netherlands and Belgium, was a hub of the northern Renaissance. Ideas from Italy had traveled across Europe–largely thanks to the movable-type printing press, invented in Germany in the 1440s. Mass-produced books meant that cultural thinking could spread like never before.

The Rhinoceros, Albrecht Dürer, 1515

Look Closer

Dürer's print circulated Europe and shaped people's idea of a rhinoceros for more than two hundred years! What did he get wrong in this image?

The Power of Print

Dürer saw the early potential of printmaking. He began engraving designs on wood or metal, printing multiple copies, publishing some, and selling them far and wide. By his mid-20s, he was the first truly international artist. After making his rhino drawing, he turned it into a woodcut, printed it cheaply, and sold it like a piece of illustrated news.

Self Importance

Dürer traveled twice to Italy, enjoying the high status that great artists held there. He painted several self-portraits. In this one below, he elevated himself to a front-on pose that was usually reserved for Christ. As with all his work, he signed this with a monogram of his initials, making sure that everyone knew his name.

Self-Portrait, Albrecht Dürer, 1500

Church and More **Change**

The thriving Renaissance in northern Europe took a dramatic turn in the 1520s. Just as people had challenged the Catholic Church in Italy, they did so here, but in a more extreme form. This became known as the Reformation.

Garden of Earthly Delights, Hieronymus Bosch, c.1490–1500

The Reformation

A German monk named Martin Luther drove the Reformation. He resented the way the Catholic Church took money, known as indulgences, to redeem people if they sinned. Luther believed that people should earn their forgiveness from God, not the pope, by doing good deeds. His ideas led to the split of the Christian Church into Catholics and Protestants.

Religious Change

Indulgences were a lucrative business that paid for religious art commissions, including many of the lavish projects in Rome. But as the Protestant faith began to dominate Northern Europe, far less sacred art was made. Paintings such as this contrasting vision of paradise and hell (above) by Hieronymus Bosch made way for more secular and humanist subjects.

Human Power

Hans Holbein the Younger captured the spirit of the Reformation in this portrait at right of a French ambassador and bishop. The books and instruments show them as knowledgeable men. They were living at a time when scientists were discovering more about the Earth and the universe. In front of all their worldly wisdom, a distorted skull reminds us of the certainty of death.

The Ambassadors, Hans Holbein the Younger, 1533

Look Closer

The skull only becomes clear when you view it from the far right of the painting. At this point, everything else looks like a blur. Why do you think Holbein painted it like this?

Children's Games, Pieter Bruegel the Elder, 1560

Everyday Subject

Most of the images we've seen so far show religious, classical, or wealthy figures. But the Flemish artist Pieter Breugel the Elder painted ordinary people. He worked for both Catholic and Protestant patrons, and his pictures usually had a moral. This one above showing children—a rare subject—may suggest that children are equal to adults in the eyes of God.

Look Closer

There are more than 200 children playing over 80 games in this painting! What can you spot?

The Stylish Style

While the Reformation threw Northern Europe into turmoil, wars were waging across Italy too. Perhaps it was these unsettled times that led to a shake-up in art style. From 1520 a movement called mannerism gave art an anxious new look.

Style and Status

The word *mannerism* comes from *maniera*, meaning "style," and is sometimes called the "stylish style." This is because the mannerists self-consciously made their paintings a certain way rather than copying nature. They wanted ideas and intellect to be at the forefront of their work. This corresponded with the new higher status of artists in society.

Twisting Trends

Mannerist art was fanciful and surprising, with elongated figures and other exaggerated effects. But rather than breaking from High Renaissance trends, it took them in a new direction. The mannerists admired Michelangelo in particular for tackling difficult, twisted poses. They respected Raphael's graceful drama but made it more extreme.

Madonna with the Long Neck, Girolamo Mazzola (Parmigianino), c. 1535

The Annunciation, El Greco, 1597–1600

Crammed Composition

Parmigianino's painting (far left) shows the Virgin Mary with a long, swanlike neck and small head. A group of angels are crammed to the left of her, admiring an oversized baby Jesus. Meanwhile a miniature St. Jerome looks lost in the wide space to the right. There is little sense of depth with everyone up close. All this imbalance is typical of mannerism.

Emotional Effect

Mannerism spread from Italy to other parts of Europe. In Spain, Doménikos Theotokópolous (El Greco) used the style to show emotion. As you can see in the painting at left, his colors and lighting were garish, giving a haunting feel. The unnatural figures, visible brushstrokes, and irrational perspective were shocking for people used to the ideals of Renaissance art.

41

Renaissance Women

Today anyone can learn to paint. But in Renaissance times, female artists were rare. Only a few women made their name as painters against the odds in a male-dominated world.

Man's World

The women who did learn art usually had wealthy or master-artist fathers. Even the life models in Renaissance workshops were men, so for an artist to draw a woman, he had to adapt what he saw. It was unacceptable for women to look at nudes, which prevented them from studying anatomy. Most paintings by female Renaissance artists are portraits.

Game of Chess, Sofonisba Anguissola, 1555

Lively Portraits

Sofonisba Anguissola was lucky that her father encouraged her to paint. Living in Italy, she traveled to Rome where Michelangelo recognized her talent. This portrait (above) of three of her sisters is striking for their expressions, which are unusually lighthearted for the time. Sofonisba was one of the first professional female artists and went on to paint at the court of Philip II of Spain.

Flemish Miniatures

The Flemish painter Levina Teerlinc was taught by her artist father. He was an illustrator of manuscripts, and she became known for her intricate portrait miniatures. This one at right shows a young Elizabeth I, daughter of Henry VIII of England. Teerlinc served as royal painter to Henry VIII, following in the footsteps of Hans Holbein the Younger.

Princess Elizabeth Tudor,
Levina Teerlinc, c. 1550–51

Still Life, Fede Galizia, c. 1507

Still Life Pioneer

Fede Galizia, an Italian painter, also learned from her father. As well as painting excellent portraits, she produced more than 40 still lifes like the one above. Still life was quite a new genre in the 16th century, and Galizia was a pioneer. She painted arrangements of fruit in skillful detail, with attention to texture, light, and shade.

A Lasting Legacy

Wars across Europe and religious crisis were the downfall of the Renaissance. Money became tight and free thinking was stifled. But even though art began to move in new directions, no one forgot what had been achieved.

Baroque Drama

Halfway through the 16th century, the popes in Italy fought back against the Reformation. Trying to win support, they commissioned new art that they hoped ordinary people would understand. A new style called Baroque emerged, with artists like Michelangelo Merisi di Caravaggio painting theatrical religious scenes. They used Renaissance skills, including chiaroscuro, but injected more realism and drama.

Look Closer

Caravaggio is known for his dramatic chiaroscuro. How does he use light to help tell the story of Christ calling St. Matthew in this painting at right?

The Calling of St. Matthew, Caravaggio, c. 1599–1600

Seated Woman, Pablo Picasso, 1920

A Lasting Legacy

The impact of the Renaissance snowballed over the centuries. Many modern artists, from Pablo Picasso (left) to the pavement painter Kurt Wenner, have revisited classical themes. Artists learn perspective, oil painting, and other 15th-century techniques in their training. Even those rebelling against Renaissance ideas are affected by them in their own way.

Ubiquitous Icons

Leonardo da Vinci and Michelangelo were well known in their day, but they are even more famous now. People flock to see their work in galleries and museums or buy copies of it on postcards, calendars, clothes, and other objects. Andy Warhol commented on this when he created his *Colored Mona Lisa* (below). He showed the legendary portrait as a mass-produced piece of art.

Colored Mona Lisa, Andy Warhol, 1963

Changing the world

The Renaissance was a period of great innovation, not only in art but in science and other areas too. European explorers discovered new lands, astronomers found that Earth orbits the sun, and the printing press helped all this news to spread around the globe. In many ways, the Renaissance was the making of the modern world and sowed seeds for the creative thinking of the future.

Glossary

anatomy–the workings of the human (or animal) body

apprentice–someone learning a trade from a skilled employer

canvas–a strong type of fabric that many artists use to paint on, especially in oils

chiaroscuro–a technique that uses light and shadow to highlight certain areas of a painting

classical–relating to ancient Greek and Roman culture

commission–to order and pay for something to be made

composition–the way parts of a picture or sculpture are arranged

court artist–an artist who worked for a royal or noble family

engraving–a print made from an engraved design

equestrian–to do with horses

etch–to engrave a design

foreshorten–to paint something shorter than it really is, so it appears to be receding into space

fresco–a type of wall painting

glaze–a very thin coating, for example of oil paint

gold leaf–gold that has been beaten into very thin sheets

humanism–belief in the importance of human nature as opposed to supernatural or religious ideas

iconic–widely recognized

idealized–made to look more perfect than reality

illusion–something that tricks the eye or isn't what it seems

medieval–relating to the Middle Ages, the period from c. 500 to the 1450s

monogram–a symbol made from interwoven letters

moral–a meaning, or lesson to be learned

mural–a painting made directly onto a wall

myth–a traditional story

naturalism–depicting realistic things or people in a natural setting

nymph–a mythical spirit of nature, appearing as a beautiful woman

patron–a person who supports someone financially, for example by commissioning an artist to make art

perspective–the art of showing three-dimensional objects on a flat surface, creating the effect of depth and distance

pigment–a type of coloring, usually in powdered form, that forms the basis of paint

plague–a highly contagious deadly disease

relief–a wall-mounted sculpture, like a 3D picture, with elements raised from a flat base

Roman Empire–a huge territory, at one time stretching over millions of kilometers, ruled by Rome from 27 BCE until the 5th century CE when it was split into the Eastern and Western Empires

scale–the relative size of something

sfumato–using a smoky effect, where the edges are blurred

sketch–a rough drawing, done in preparation for a finished work

still life–a painting or drawing of an arrangement of objects, such as fruit in a bowl or flowers in a vase

studio–an artist's workplace

stylized–shown in a consciously artistic way, rather than being realistic

tempera–paint made from pigments mixed with a water-soluble binder, such as egg yolk

texture–the feel of a surface, such as rough brick or smooth glass

woodcut print–a print made by carving a design into a block of wood, covering it in paint or ink, and pressing it on to a surface

Read More

Books

Agrimbau, Diego. *Leonardo da Vinci.* North Mankato, Minn.: Capstone Press, 2018.

Carr, Simonetta. *Michelangelo for Kids: His Life and Ideas, with 21 Activities.* Chicago: Chicago Review Press, 2016.

Internet Sites

Kids Discover: Renaissance *https://online.kidsdiscover.com/unit/ renaissance?ReturnUrl=/unit/renaissance*

The National Gallery: Tour Renaissance Masterpieces *www.nationalgallery.org.uk/paintings/tour-renaissance-masterpieces*

Renaissance in Italy: 1400s *www.kahnacademy.org/humanities/ renaissance-reformation/early-renaissance1*

Timeline

1304 Giotto begins his frescoes at the Arena Chapel in Padua, including *Betrayal of Christ*. He starts to evolve the flat medieval painting style into something more lifelike and 3D.

1309 The popes move from Rome and make their base in Avignon, France.

1338 Lorenzetti introduces secular painting with his government frescoes in Siena.

1377 Pope Gregory XI moves his court back to Rome. This ends the Avignon Papacy, but leads to decades of conflict over who should be pope and where.

1401 The Cloth Merchants Guild holds a competition to design the north doors of the Florence Baptistery. Ghiberti wins.

1412 The Medici family of Florence become official bankers to the Papacy.

1420 Brunelleschi designs his Florence Cathedral dome.

1434 Van Eyck paints his *Arnolfini Portrait*, one of the first masterpieces in oils.

1435 Alberti writes *Della Pittura (On Painting)*, which explains how to use Brunelleschi's system of linear perspective.

c. 1440 Donatello sculpts his bronze *David*, the first statue of a nude figure since antiquity. The German Johannes Gutenberg invents the printing press.

1452 Ghiberti completes his second set of Baptistery doors.

c. 1455 The first printed book, the *Gutenberg Bible*, is published in Germany.

1466 A young Leonardo da Vinci is apprenticed to Verrocchio in Florence.

1484 Dürer creates his first self-portrait at the age of 13.

1490 Michelangelo moves in to the Medici Palace, where he lives and studies for two years. The period known as the High Renaissance begins.

1494 Michelangelo flees Florence when the friar Savonarola seizes control from the ruling Medici.

1501 Michelangelo returns to Florence, where he begins work on his statue of David.

1503 Pope Julius II comes to power and commissions artists and architects to restore and beautify Rome.

1506 Leonardo completes the *Mona Lisa*.

1507 Titian joins the workshop of Giovanni Bellini in Venice. He is also heavily influenced by Giorgione.

1508 Raphael moves to Rome to help decorate the Vatican Palace. Michelangelo, already there, starts painting the Sistine Chapel Ceiling.

1515 Dürer creates his *Rhinoceros* print.

1517 Martin Luther begins the Reformation, which leads to the founding of the Protestant Church.

1519 Leonardo dies in France.

1527 Rome is invaded by Charles V, leader of the Holy Roman Empire (a collection of territories in central Europe). Many artists flee the city.

1528 Dürer dies in Germany.

c. 1535 Parmigianino paints his *Madonna With the Long Neck*, a pinnacle of the mannerist style that followed the High Renaissance.

1550 Giorgio Vasari publishes *The Lives of the Most Excellent Painters, Sculptors and Architects*, a book about many of the great Renaissance artists.

1550s–60s Pieter Bruegel the Elder paints scenes of ordinary villagers.

1564 Michelangelo dies in Rome.

1576 Titian dies in Venice.

1590s Caravaggio makes some of the first Baroque paintings.

Index